BURNING THE YEARS

and

LOBO

POEMS 1962 - 1975

By

WILLIAM CHILDRESS

Library of Congress Catalog Card Number: 86-81734

BURNING THE YEARS/LOBO
Copyright: William Childress 1986. All rights reserved.

ISBN 0-9607958-4-7 Hardback
ISBN 0-9607958-5-5 Paperback

Printed in the United States of America

Essai Seay Publications
P.O. Box 55
East St. Louis, IL 62202
U.S.A.

This book is dedicted to my sons

Christopher Brandon Childress
Jason William Childress
David Daniel Childress
whom I love.

INTRODUCTION

Most folks who know me, if they know of me at all, are readers of my *ST. LOUIS POST-DISPATCH* column, "Out of the Ozarks." Many letters have kindly commented on the poetic nature of some of those columns. So, for those men and women who enjoy poetry, Essai Seay Publications republishes my two books of poems from the early 1970's.

In these books, however, you will find a more serious poet, a younger writer not quite sure the world is all he'd like it to be.

Because some of the poetry is bleak, I talked with Publisher Sheryl Clayton at some length. "Do we really want to include the more graphic poems—the poems of war and madness?" I asked. "There are many poems that take a gentler view of things," I continued.

Her reply was to the point. "All of those poems show your development as a poet and writer," she said. "They represent what you wrote about then—and we don't want to rob the reader of coming in contact with that aspect of you."

So, all of the poems in my first book, *BURNING THE YEARS* as well as all those from my second book, *LOBO*, are here.

In a departure from most poetry books, I've made comments about many of the poems, including what I thought and felt when I wrote them; the locale, the meter, the rhyme, if any, and the technical aspects of the poem's construction.

To folks who are used to simpler verse, talking about "syllabics" or "slant rhyme" or "symbolism" will open a new pathway—and will make the book potentially useful as a supplementary text.

But confusing the "poetic voice," which is in each poem, with the poet himself won't work. I am me—and the voice is the voice. Poets need to be crazy, and there is proof in the voices we hear as we write our poems. That's what Shakespeare meant

when he said, "The poet's eye, in a fine frenzy roll-
ing..." (Act 5, Scene 1, A Midsummer Night's
Dream).

Hopefully, afterwards we return to sanity.

Not all of these poems will suit you. But I think
you'll remember some of them for a long time.

BURNING THE YEARS (First published in 1971
by *THE SMITH*). It's hard to say anything signifi-
cant about "Hiroshima," the first poem in this
book. It is long, and is based closely on John Her-
sey's fine book of the same name, and won the
$1000 Stephen Vincent Benet Award in 1979.

The poem, written while I was an editor-writer
at National Geographic in Washington, D.C. takes
the viewpoint of different, but very real people
who lived in Hiroshima when the atomic bomb fell.
Through their eyes we relive the horror and the
agony of the first atomic bomb dropped by man
upon his fellow man. My typist (age 16) loves this
poem.

One note of interest: I tried to write a haiku for
the tiny section called, "The Haiku Poet." But, I
could never get quite what I wanted. Then, in one
of those lovely serendipities that sometimes happen
in life, I came across the work of Kobayashi Issa,
one of the great haiku poets—still much treasured—
of feudal Japan.

His haiku seemed to depict an atomic-bombed
horse so perfectly, I used it at once—feeling at the
same time how strange is history, that a poet from
200 years ago could be so prophetic.

The other poems in *BURNING THE YEARS* will
have notes with the poems.

LOBO (First published in 1972 by Barlenmir
House, now defunct).

In manuscript, *LOBO* was the unanimous choice
of the Devins Award judges out of 369 manuscripts
submitted nationally in 1971. The award was
sponsored by the Jewish Community Center in
Kansas City. I proudly flew there at my expense to

accept it. The Devins apparently no longer exists, but in the early 1970s it was prestigious, and carried a cash award of $500 plus publication by a university press. One of my favorite poets, William Stafford, presented the award.

I had barely returned to California when someone at the press raised a hue and cry about "legitimacy." *LOBO* contained some poems that had appeared in *BURING THE YEARS* and this person, a former military criminal investigative type, had brought their crime-cracking powers to bear.

THE SMITH, still a lively literary magazine in New York—fired off a telegram saying the poems in *BURNING THE YEARS* should be excused because they were part of their special magazine issues and in magazine format. The press was unmoved.

William Stafford, remarkable politician, as well as a fine poet, declined to get involved—but E.V. Griffith of the top flight publication *POETRY NOW* wrote a letter in my behalf. The Devins people were in a quandary. They did not want their award "compromised".

In the end, it was decided that *LOBO* would receive "A" but not "THE" Devins Award. I received $500 but my book was not published by the university press.

Looking back 15 years, the whole thing is now funny. But, as a hungry poet, the accusation hurt, and the possible loss of money hurt even more. I've never made this public before—I just wanted to share a "tempest in a teapot" with my readers.

With this book, you hold 20 years of my life in your hands. I've enjoyed those years. I hope you will too.

— William Childress
W. C.'s Fields
Anderson, MO 64831
Arpil 1, 1986

HIROSHIMA

I. THE RAYON MAN

The blossoms hang heavy in my garden,
red as embers, luring the amber bees.
Yesterday there were small bright
birds, darting and singing,
singing of the death that will come.

Each day the dark wings of war
shadow Hiroshima, and move on
to other cities. I, the Rayon Man,
maker of fabrics, believe our escape
foreshadows an end more terrible

than any known, and the rubble
of Hiroshima will scar the world.
August is a time for life, not death,
but war has so calloused my eyes
I can no longer see tomorrow.

The early sun is like warm breath,
but it cannot melt the sorrow
freezing my heart. My only son,
a soldier, has fallen in Singapore.
Far away, I hear a train mourning.

Beside the gate my kinsmen search
the skies, nerves fluttering like flags.
The day my son went away, the flame
in my stone lantern went with him,
and a golden carp rose, bellyup, in my pond.

There is a spirit moving in my garden.
I feel my son's presence on the wind.
I see him, a child with Miharu Kinma,
his toy horse, long since laid away.
Why did a child die and a man emerge?

II. THE PRIEST

Already August and five days flown,
and now it is the morning of the sixth day.
On that day, God finished his creation
and gave it to man to destroy. Strange—
I'm still not used to the baritones
of planes, like those three B-29's...

I am a priest and a German,
and I have no place here. Starving
on rice gruel, an alien in an alien race,
I cling to faith like the Japanese to face.
Death does not matter; only disgrace.

Well, Deus vult, this is my chosen life
if I can keep it in these days of strife.
Ah—the planes are going away.
Dei gratias, the all-clear is sounding.
MERCIFUL GOD! THE SKY IS FLAMING!
(Is that me screaming?)

III. MRS. ISAWA NAKAMURA

It's eight o'clock, my husband.
The children are playing in the garden.
I have sent your mother to Nagasaki
where she will be safe. Now I am alone
with your ghost, remembering your words.

You said: "I, Isawa Nakamura, Tailor,
have been called to serve my Emperor. Wife,
take care of our children. Children,
love and obey your mother, and I
will send you gifts from Singapore."

The wind picked your words to bones,
and this morning, my tears break the sun
into many suns. Singapore's only gift
was your funeral urn, which sits now
in your ancestral shrine.

Ai! What is the light, that wind?
O, THE HEAVENS ARE BURNING!
Ai, shu Jesusu awaremi tamai!
The children, where are the children?
Toshio!   Yaeko!   Myeko!
O, my husband, it grows dark...

IV. Tanimoto

I was moving a *tansu,*
a cabinet, when the blue
day broke open, and its fiery
innards erupted like Fujiyama.
The earth rose and struck me.

When I woke, I saw clouds dappled
with strange lights—and the severed
head of a soldier staring at me,
pierced by a metal sliver
like a stick in a candy apple.

A woman with a bleeding face
crooned to a bloody bundle,
her infant son—dead in the first
instant of terrible fire.

After the fierce light, dusk fell.
Burned people stumbled towards a river
choked with bodies and hidden by smoke.
Winds roared as though from Hell.
Dust boiled upward, grey and thick.

There were scenes no man should remember.
Blindly circling, a girl whose raw skin
flapped like rags reached out her hands
and cried *Tasukete, tasukete!* But no one
could help her that day in Hiroshima.

Blistered mouths begged *Mizu, mizu,*
but there was no water.

An old man with bleeding eyes
raved that Hiroshima had become the sun,
that the sky was full of fire.

Slowly, the living became the dead.
near Dobashi Bridge I found a boat
and set out to save those I could.
The flames drove many to drown.
Corpses bobbed on the current.

Like the dark backs of cormorants.
I reached for a young girl's hands,
and the flesh slid off like gloves.
She stared at the wet, pink bones
without making a sound.

Far up the river, despairing cries
echoed—like birds, caught in a net,
the fiery net of Hiroshima.
I heard a woman on the shore
calling *Toshio, Yaeko, Myeko.*
No one answered.

V. THE FISHERMAN

I, Kurin Tanabe, was guiding my boat
on the Inland Sea, near Tsuzu
when the sun fell and the bright
sky became a net filled with fire.

The noise made my ears cry in pain.
In the water, hordes of fishes
splintered into the depths like broken
mirrors. Great drops of rain fell.

The fish fled in long, bright lines,
seeking safety deep in the ocean
like birds fleeing a storm.
No one will catch fish here again.

VI. THE HAIKU POET

A sudden shower
    And I am riding naked
        on a naked horse.

VII. THE RAYON MAN

The terrible winds
burned and tore us,
hurled us skyward
like paper kites.
A child flew past
in a cloud of fire.

Flames roofed my house
with fierce, bright cloth.
The carp in my pond
boiled to golden froth,
and burned horses
passed my gate in agony,

their melted eyes
leaking jellied tears.
Thin blue milk
trickled from
the seared udders
of dying mares.

Rivers of fire
lapped distant hills
like bright water,
and broken glass shone
like dead eyes in the grey dusk.

I saw children whose flesh
hung like crimson kimonos,
Hiroshima's children,
branded forever,
branded that all
would see and remember.

Now I stand among the ruins
of my ancestral temple.
Soon I will be with my son.
already the strange sickness
burns my bones. *Shikata ga nai,*
I am past caring. I am alone
since Hiroshima became the sun.

VIII. Mrs. Nakamura

My husband,
if only you were here
to sew shut my eyes.
I can no longer
face this landscape, so bare
of the green life
it once knew.

Perhaps the flowers
will grow again
on these hills,
and the green grass come back,
but so many flowers
are now gone forever.

Toshio, Yaeko, Myeko,
are one with the winds.
Wearing their kimono petals,
they fled like summer blossoms,
or like the cinders
of blossoms.

I have come
to mingle my ashes with yours,
my husband.
Temple, shelter
our souls forever.
SAYONARA.

I've never had any luck with green-thumbing, and vastly admire
folks who can make things grow. Only in one instance did I luck out,
when I casually tossed some zinnia seeds by the steps of a ranch
house. It was late in the year, but those wonderful flowers just kept
on growing. And so I began to see in them some great significance,
even a tiny model of our universal selves. This began as an iambic
pentameter sonnet, but Philip Levine told me that last two lines
added nothing — so I clipped them, leaving only 12 lines, not the
required 14.

FLORAL TRIBUTE

Winter comes with all a winter's promise,
and still the flowers bloom by my front door.
I dropped their seeds as late as late September,
and now they face December with a calmness
denied by their stiff stance against my wall.
I ask if they feel pain when, winter tossed,
their rigid leaves are tentacled by frost,
or what they feel, or if they feel at all.
My flowers give no warmth and ask for none:
each petal surrounds its own consistent sun
in perfect symmetry. I have known worse
arrangements that were called a universe.

This little poem grew out of my ranch foreman days on a rich miser's ranch near Clovis, California. It was a country place, with advantages other than money or housing and I was young, lean, and didn't worry much about anything. The poet and fine banjoist Peter Everwine, one of my writing teachers, hunted pheasant here with me once. We both shot at the same bird, but he insisted he got it. I still think I did. More truthfully, probably we both did.

AUTUMN EQUINOX

Dust-devils coil in the yellow sky,
and the sun hangs like a Chinese gong.
From the field, a solitary quail
erupts with tiny thunder, flying
to thicker grain for its evening meal.
Far away, I hear a bluejay cry.

In wooden flower boxes, blossoms
planted late wilt in the autumn heat,
their stems coiled like the hose
on my lawn, while trellised vines
try to recall the summer season
by bringing forth a final rose.

My year in juvenile hall as a counselor was heart-rending in many ways. More than anything, it started me to thinking about the licensing of parents—allowing the authorities to specify who should have children on the basis of mental stability, an ability to support the children, and other social factors. Illegitimate and problem children are a grave social burden, but the worst suffering is among the children. If I were to be born only to suffer at the hands of parents too ignorant or unstable to care, I'd rather not be born. China is severely limiting births now. But we are a free nation, and not yet willing to face alternative social possibilities which might benefit both worthwhile parents—and as yet unborn children.

JUVENILE HALL AT NIGHT

My flashlight probes
the dark rooms where childhood, denied by day,
returns in sleep. Their
faces are more open
when their eyes are closed,
but each expression
holds dreams
that are darker
than bruises.
For the little I can do
at this late hour,
their lives are placed in my keeping.
I am their temporary father,
they are my momentary sons,
yet I am their prisoner
far more than they
are mine.

This and one other poem were written at the birth of my first son. The original date was 1967, made 1970 for the anthology. A black friend in my poetry writing classes at the U. of Iowa was the only one who defended this poem when it was "dissected" by our fellow students. It is a bitter poem, in which the poet tries to adopt a Negro persona for those days were filled with bitterness and violence as Blacks tried to move upward and a deadly war took its toll of both white and black. Drugs were also rife.

NOTE FROM A PART-TIME NEGRO

1970:   Paranoid,
I tear another year from my life
and stare at the fog that hides the dirt
beyond my window. A room away, my wife
sleeps and dreams of spiders, pregnant
with another number for IBM.
The child will be born a natural card,
under Aries, the sign of the ram.
I would weep for it if I could weep,
but tears are as sporadic as sleep
anymore, and as a rule induced
only by country clubs and tear gas,
or my numbered days on calendars.
Yes, I'm sick, but no more than those
who write in toilets, "Nixon eats Niggers."
A little grass, some acid, I make my way,
and every year become a little larger.

I wrote quite a few poems while at National Geographic, most long since published, and one—"Hiroshima"—a prizewinner. I called them, for the most part, my "paranoia poems." Here is one, and it is funny or not, depending on your sense of humor.

WHISTLING IN D.C.

Whistling on 17th
near DeSales, all in
my Geographic clothes,
I saw eyes grow hard,
grow cold, grow angry.

Remember your loved ones!
snarled a flower seller,
as an empty sleeve
flapped past crying,
Why weren't you in Viet Nam?

Much worse was
the mini-skirted blonde
whose flopping big jugs
shrieked Rapist!

as a night stick
fell from a cop
and the sidewalk kissed me.

I sit in this cell fully apprised of my rights
as man and citizen.
But they can't con me.
When I get out, nothing will
ever again persuade me
to whistle in D.C.

If you're ever in Washington, by all means visit the National Geographic Museum. It is a nifty place, and has the first space capsule, and bizarre amphibians, and lots of men in 3-piece suits. Say hello to my dear old office mate, David Robinson, while there. We are still close despite his Republican ways. This is another "paranoia poem," but the frog was real—and huge.

THE GIANT FROG

In the National Geographic museum,
there is a giant frog
suspended behind glass
in the chemicals of science,
he sprawls like a green crucifixion.

I must now call your attention
to my eyes: Notice how
they have grown larger,
how they tend to pooch out
like those of my stunned friend

late of the Rio Muni in Africa?
I am paid to keep up inward
appearances, while the fluid
they have put in his tank
only preserves his exterior.

And now, if you'll excuse me,
I must go and ask the guard
if he will let me out for awhile.
Taking care with my webbed
feet on the stairs, spearing
stray insects with my tongue.

BURNING THE YEARS, 1971

In 1963 when I wrote this poem as an undergraduate at Fresno State College, I ran a small ranch for a man who was to pennies what rust is to hinges. He was so tight he squeaked when he walked, but students are used to being taken advantage of—so I took his $40 a month and decrepit house and made do. But O.G.S. is surely wealthy today, because he didn't waste any money on his employees.

THE CAPTIVE

To find a small, private place
was his dream, there to create
things of beauty if he could.
He found it. Wind burned his face.
He sat on an apple crate
and wrote verses made of wood.
Working for a rich man,
he remained poor. The country place
he cared for did not care for him.
The plumbing failed; the roof
let in the rain, and he had proof
if he should ever need it
that hard work made the man.
But no, someone had lied
and he had believed. That year,
the cattle succumbed to bloat
and fences fell. The owner wrote
that he was dissatisfied.
Days followed in succession
like tears down dusty cheeks.
At the barbed-wire barricade,
cattled lowed for food. The weeks
of drought brought only locust
clouds, while all that he had made
could only undo his dreams.
He watched the aimless circling
of pigeons over the barn
saw the sun coat the burning
hills with rust, and setting,
sew shut the day's raw, red seams.

BURNING THE YEARS, book, 1971—a poem about revisiting scenes of childhood while on a freelance magazine trip in the late 1960s. I spent a night in jail in Bisbee, AZ.

BISBEE, ARIZONA

Tailings rise like chalk cliffs,
Arizona's Dover, recalling the
copper days when dusty gnomes
rose from the pits in ore cars,
the thin commas of their carbide
lamps giving the darkness pause.

In Bisbee, I helped reelect
a Sheriff by playing desperado
to his Earp. The mistake was his,
but so was the gun, no less real
for being nickelplated. Who can
write the importance of being

Sheriff of Bisbee? Next morning
they told me to light out and not
look back. In the desert, bent
saguaros waved me on. There are
no faces in Bisbee. Just blank
postcards cancelled by time.

GLOBE, ARIZONA

West of town, Sleeping Beauty
spills her mountain tresses.
The Old Dominion Mine, gutted
by underground rivers, still lifts
its broken slag heaps to the sky.
People talk of lost riches,
of enough copper to build
a copper city, and never mention
the drowned miners rotting below.

On a hillside, I visit the fallen
walls and broken windows
of childhood. Someone has scrawled
Jedd Fukt Bonnie Heer. A lizard
blinks from a crevice. The pond
my father built is filled with
shale, cairns for the goldfish
and for him. Only the sun is the same,
blistering the paint on my car.

CLAYPOOL, ARIZONA

South toward Phoenix,
past the Reservation
where muscatel bottles,
the White Man's golden gift
to the Indians, flash among
ocatillo; rising past fossil
villages where tourists grovel
for pottery shards to decorate

their own fragmented lives;
descending past a graveyard
where no Indians are buried.
Claypool: here I meet a boyhood
memory, grown fat and myopic.
He calendars back the years
to a distant face, studies
the lines no pen has written

and wonder that they tell
as much as they do. That night,
we trek the rock strewn hills,
and wonder why the years
have stampeded like mustangs.
Our campfire is only one star
among many. By dawn it is out,
leaving us hunched and cold.

While at the University of Iowa Writer's Workshop, the granddaddy of them all, I decided I wanted to get into being an American Indian poet—so I took the pretentious name Young Hawk. This made my long time friend E.V. Griffith of Poetry Now laugh so hard, he sent me the bill for his hernia. "Young Hawk"—quite a jump since I'm of Danish extraction—produced half a dozen poems at most before going to the Happy Hunting Grounds. This one appeared as credited above. All were published.

DESERT SPRING NIGHT

The desert in the rains of spring
is like that shining, unstrung water,
and if you have an Apache's patience,
you can sit at night afterward,
alone in the wetness, and be the blue
hesitant opening of Angel's Breath.
Be also the scarlet flowers of Cholla,
the bright, brief flame of saguaro,
and the crimson fur of ocatillo.
And here in all this life, be the little
deaths of little things; the grinding
cry of a rabbit taloned by a hawk,
the chalk-squeak of kangaroo rats.
Such is my desert, austere in the sun.
Its only beauty burns in darkness,
and the weak creatures dormant in its day
only sleep more deeply in its night.

BURNING THE YEARS, book, 1971

My family lived in Arizona twice, as befits gypsying migrant cotton pickers. Dad worked in the coppermines during World War 2, and the town was near an Apache Indian Reservation. I became a regular visitor, a tow-headed kid of ten, greatly curious of Indian ways. They were a very tolerant people, who obviously loved children—else they'd have run me off. Many years later I romanticized what was, as I look back, a bleak and poverty-stricken way of life.

ANTELOPE CHILD

Hell is the southwestern
desert in August;
the crack of wind
against hot rocks,
the birds who won't light
for fear their feet
will remain.
It is the lime-green
of Spanish daggers
peeled and split
by the sun; air that
burns the lungs like smoke,
and hollow rocks
where stagnant water simmers.

It was here in such summers
that I ran,
a brown child
mocking the desert
antelope, nor was I part
of the white and pampered
world,
for I was wild.
In a hut of dry withes,
my fat mother
and somber father
fed me stewed coyote,
and I grew.
Nothing more need be said.

BURNING THE YEARS, book, 1971

At the time I was "Young Hawk", an Indian poet, I was also reading a lot of "Indian" lore like Don Juan, Adventures of a Yaqui Indian (or some such title). Mysticism and drugs were an equal mix in these books, and of course peyote and "magic mushrooms" figured in many religious ceremonies of desert tribes. Perhaps for its monotonic rhythms and "mind blowing" aspects, I like this little poem, now almost 20 years old.

APACHE

Mescalero I am,
Athapascan I speak,
a language as dead
as my people are dying.
I ran as a youth
past the Reservations's bounds,
only finding it again
as a man. For garden,
the desert, for walls,
the hills, and beyond,
horizons as wide as the sun.
A nomad for decades,
I saw many things,
but the red, severed gorges
still bled in my dreams
and the serrated ridges
near the hut I was born in
were the clouds
of each moonrise,
the flesh
of each sunrise.
So I went back one time,
but the hut had decayed,
and the hard earth grew
only jade prickly-pear.
And I ate the sweet buds
of that green plant,
and the walls fell again
and again I was gone.

Spiders repulse and fascinate me. They are such efficient executioners. They have such power over lesser creatures. Small wonder, then, that I would be inclined to think of them in terms of some ultimate power. A creepy free verse effort from student days.

THE SPIDER'S COMMUNION

I haven't time to tell you
what went wrong in that long ago Eden,
or why we were driven out
to make our way, bobbing and weaving,
casting shining nets,
silent and strong.

I haven't time to tell you
(since I must hunt)
how we earn all we eat
by hard work and cautious planning.
I have no time for your questions,
no time, no time!

Our Satan might have been
a hunting wasp, sent for that
sinful moment when we fell in unison,
although only one of us
savored to the fullest
that despairing fall.

Ah, it was sweet in the garden,
sweet in the way
only life-giving fluids can be.
A thing would lose its life
that we might gain it,
for we lost, we lost, we lost!
Among all those flowers,
ours was the strangest nectar.

But I have no time.
Always, I begin the hunt with a song
and a tiny sacrifice:
the dried husks of whatever
is in my nest. Then I offer a
prayer to God,
who has eight legs,
and fangs like surgical needles,
and watches over those of us
who are created in His image.

I think this was among several poems I had in the late 1960s in
"The Reporter", a fine and literate magazine which ceased publishing
a few years later.

The poem is about a furlough I took just before being shipped to
the Korean War in 1952.

SOLDIER'S LEAVE

Beside the river where he walks
boulders like green and moldy loaves
resist the downward pull of water
and hold their own in ordered grooves.

It is October, and the leaves,
once so flexible and green
grate on each other in the wind
like a surgeon's knife on bone.

Soon ice will form among the trees
in lean cinereous splinters,
but he will be gone before it does
on a cold campaign of winter's.

POETRY MAGAZINE, 1962

The original poem was three times this long, but space is precious in poetry magazines, so when Henry Rago offered to publish the first part I leaped at the chance. *Poetry Magazine* was the top publication of the day, and my poetry teacher, Phil Levine, was delighted that the poem had been accepted. I'm indebted to Phil for the line, "Beyond human praise."

THE SOLDIERS

In Korea, decomposing shit
chokes the perfume of the stray flower
still seen occasionally on hills,
and the paddies heavily seeded
with napalm mines, can grow red flowers
at a touch, with a blossom that kills.

From the dark immobilization
of earth bunkers, our probing patrol
infiltrates forests. Distant searchlights
paint ridges with something like moonlight,
and a grey rain chills us. Winter's cold
is not far away. It too will come.

Our ghosts meet other ghosts in the trees:
They appear pallid and luminous
in the eyepiece of a sniperscope,
a tool too complex for the Chinese.
But their simple burpguns never stop,
and their simple power murders us.

In December we start pulling out,
having done little but christen hills
with proper names: Million Dollar,
Triangle, Heartbreak; names that matter
to no one but us. We taste defeat
and like it. Victory is what kills.

No soldier can ignore tomorrow,
though finally it does not matter
as much as it should. We have today,
and by the grace of Generals a stay
of execution. Our lives narrow
around living's uncertain center.

It is not likely a solution
to human problems will come of this,
but soldiers can't be soldiers and be
human. The cold rain descends softly
on scorched graves, where, beyond, human praise,
men lie in stiffened resolution.

THE FAR POINT (CANADIAN)

This is the title poem of my first book, and mirrors the beginning
of my cynical period. I, a veteran of seven years, saw Viet Nam esca-
late at the hands of Lyndon Baines Johnson. The day he ordered the
air strike I begged my wife to stay home because I was sure there'd
be H-bombs falling within hours. This free verse poem grew out of
the ritual of burning of old war pictures—photographs I wish I
had back now.

BURNING THE YEARS

Solemn as a priest, he gives
himself to fire. His shining face
wrinkles and turns brown,
a Kodak soldier
writhing in paper pain.

Goodbye to the slim youth
in paratrooper garb,
with boots like mirrors
and ribbons straight as his spine.
He knew all there was to know
about honor and duty.
But duty changes with each job,
and honor turns ashes soon enough.

Deeper in the cave of years
he's joined by man of War
who's still a boy.
Fists full of detonators and TNT,
he smiles murderously
for the folks back home.
At night he scrawls
on sweetheart letters
inscrutable Oriental signs.

Smoke rises like morning fog:
shadowy pictures, enlarged by time,
dance and preen. Girls of months or moments
feel again the fires
that once swept them and him.
but now the act is over. The fires
go out. All that's left
are the ashes in his mind.

Working in Washington, even at so exalted a job as an editor at National Geographic, made me break out in hives—and the bees were still in them. I came up with "Darvin" after "Darvon," a tranquilizer. This "city paranoia" finally resulted in my leaving town to return to college teaching. I've always like the rhyme "Garden Apt.,/something snapped" in this vers libre poem.

THE APARTMENT DWELLER

Sounds of sex or battle
reach us from the Darvins,
plastered a wall away.
He works to buy the bottle
he needs to keep on working
in Washington, D.C.

If not the Darvins, overhead
the skeletal floors clatter
as the Todds awaken the dead.
Water shrieks in the plumbing.
I wake up in sweats,
hearing bombs, hearing threats.

In our delightful Garden Apt.,
nothing grows but spiked
leaves of old rental notices.
Yesterday, something snapped
in Darvin, but Todd responded
with a robot grin, rewinding himself.

I have lived in apartments, and would rather drink croton oil three days running than do so again. This one is based on some in Oxon Hill, Maryland, a place I hope never to see again, if only because it is more suited for oxen than humans. Color this one cynical too.

THE HOUSE WITH THE NOISY CEILING

The house with the noisy ceiling
where I live with my wife and children
isn't a house at all,
but simply space enclosed
at the cheapest possible cost,
with rafters and uprights of greed
and floors of polished avarice
laid on laws that are kind to the rich.

The house with the noisy ceiling
has corners that cry in the night
like an infant weeping in hunger,
or a child abandoned by parents.
It has thin doors that curse,
walls and windows that scream,
and plaster that exhales odors,
the smells of urine and vomit.

The house with the noisy ceiling
was built by a man in Miami,
who sits in the sun by his pool,
counting his capital gains.
Righteously angry at slums,
and at people who people slums.
He writes to the President monthly
complaining of unfair taxation.

Whatever it may be today, Washington's Dupont Circle was an outdoors hodge-podge of hippies and druggies in 1969, when I wrote this sometimes exact, sometimes off-rhyme poem in tetrameter. Some interesting rhymes, and in the beginning I purposely used first-stress words to set an ominous, agressive tone.

THE PUSHER

DuPont Circle squares off at night,
giving it to the straight world straight.
Shuffling figures with arms like reeds,
pus-filled veins and eyes of paste
are making for you and making haste,
hawking their lust for wine or speed.

Gaunt black ghosts whose dismal
sermons speak of coming fear
surround the fountain. Baptismal
rites are solemnized among gowns
dark as their wearers, gentlemen
whose eyes freeze out laughter.

And then there's me, running
after whatever keeps running away.
Only I'm you, and the habit you say
you've kicked and haven't. In my eyes
the silver stalks of needles shine,
promising light for the coming day.

Richard Millstone Nixon was what we called him. He sat in the White House watching football while a quarter of a million citizens expressed their frustration and hatred of the Viet Nam War.

WASHINGTON PEACE MARCH, 1969

The sun caught D.C. off guard.
The past night's mirrors
of frozen rain still gleamed
on highways leading in.

Hunched marchers in blankets
moved like Indians on some
new trail of tears, watched
by blue cavalry on motorcycles

strangely masked.
We passed statues of heroes.
Admiral Farragut scanned the
long lines for torpedoes to damn,

his sculptured hair as long
as a hippie's. An old man rushed
the lines, fists flailing,
screaming, "You never bathe,

you never shave, you god damn
Communists!" A mother holding
a small boy shields him as she
tries to recognize a fellow

American.
Twelve abreast, quietly singing,
bearing signs saying, "Get Out
of Viet Nam Now."

The cops wouldn't meet our eyes.

All day and into the night
the columns moved, and then came
the candlelight march for all
the dead, from Arlington cemetery

to the White House and its coffins.
America passing in review,
half a million men, women, children,
an army bigger than all the sick

generals and lying politicians.
In the distance, the Washington
Monument reared over everyone
like a shining ICBM.

Over years of moving from pillar to post, I have lost—or loaned, which is the same thing—a great many books and magazines that had my work in them. I'm not a good pack rat, although I wish I was. This poem is based on a true incident, and was written when I was living in Oxon Hill, Maryland in 1970.

YOUNG CAIN

There was something loose inside him,
Something stronger than all the old warnings,
and it was telling him to kill.
Whatever it was, it was part of him,
and he was once more a child of seven,
tearing the wings off butterflies,
the better for them to reach heaven.

He had to be strong, at fifteen,
to break a woman's neck. But some
weakness kept him from smothering
the infant sleeping in its crib.
He left it to cry out its thirst
for three whole days, until death
gave it back to its mother.

And so a mother and child
die at the hands of a child.
Baltimore's streets harbor a million more,
each one immunized against pity.
And somewhere in the bestial night,
Cain is conceived on a reeking couch,
to someday set forth on his brothers.

The National Geographic building was 10 stories tall with lots of marble, if memory serves, and was generally considered (by writers) to be a mausoleum. I was amazed to be shown the office of the late Melville Bell Grosvenor, then top dog—for it had a desk elevated above where exectuives met, Melville could sit like a judge or a deity, high above the hoi polloi. One upper-level hoi was a sneery, arrogant man with a drinking problem that finally got him. On the day I left I met him in the parking lot and he said, "I'm so glad you're leaving." This is one of the Paranoia Poems about a building that kills people.

D. C. AUTUMN

Tonight I walk down
the blowing concrete canyons
past Farragut Square,
where the Admiral stands
bronzely defying torpedoes.

I think of the young girl
who worked in my office
who was too much of an individual
to last long
in such hard surroundings.

Yesterday,
in front of the building
where we work,
she turned all the colors
of autumn.

There were cries of
"What a shame!" and "Call
an ambulance!"
But only I had seen
the marble hands that pushed her.

BURNING THE YEARS, book, 1971

This is surely the supreme Paranoia Poem, or certainly it is among mine. Put yourself in a major conservative corporation full of "hawks" while you're a dove during a war that has divided a nation. Suspicion is everywhere. So is fear. So is boredom. So are spies.

IN THIS PLACE

Things are not the same.
I have ways of telling:
a deliberately dropped pencil,
the quickened snarl of Washington
six floors down,
the fidgeting of colleagues,
who change the subject
and won't look me
in the eye.

Also
in the behavior
of my secretary.
Yesterday, all day, she made no errors.
Once I caught her looking
secretive and mysterious.
The pencils on my desk
have all been sharpened.
The telephone
makes strange noises when I pick
it up
the window-washer rappels
past my glass
more swiftly than usual. And why
is there no soap
in the cleaning woman's bucket?
They're not fooling me!
I've seen all the worthwhile movies!
The note on my door
wishing me happy birthday
is a trick.

In the basement
my mail is being secretly opened.
In a nearby forest,
I hear the CIA quietly growing.

I do not know
the chairman of the board.
But last night, in the elevator,
he leaned towards me and whispered:
"Friday. Twelve o'clock."

BURNING THE YEARS, book, 1971

    When you're in the nation's capitol, you always think about how
you are supreme among H-bomb targets—perhaps one reason for
the high incidence of alcohol intake.
    Last of the Washington "paranoia poems."

WHEN THE H-BOMB FELL

When the H-Bomb fell
on Washington, I was in
THE NATIONAL GEOGRAPHIC,
in an elevator caught
at the sixth floor.

The building's top ran
down like candle wax.
I know the White House
must also have melted.

The heat was fierce.
It turned sheets of
blood, carved by flying
glass, to dark dust.

Fortunately, the elevator
was strong. I still
crouch there, among
twisted iron sculptures,
keeping my cool.

I know the diggers
from the Pentagon will
soon be here to dig
me out.

Meanwhile, I can only
hope that no one in
the White House escaped
through the clever tunnels
built at taxpayers' expense.

This poem, never sent out for publication, is the story of a marriage that slowly decays and finally dies. There is more than a hint here of the frustrations found in many marriages—which expect a relationship to be magical, wonderful, enchanting, and then cry bitter tears of disappointment when the realities of two humans living day to day, under great pressures, reveal themselves.

LOOKING FOR OZ

They had both started off
down the yellow brick road,
she a wife younger than a child,
he a husband already old
in the world's ways.
Somehow they got sidetracked
enroute to the emerald land,
and halfway there
she fell in with a cowardly lion
who led her briefly into the shadows.

Later, he found her mindlessly
frolicking with a scarecrow,
who left without saying goodbye.

Meanwhile, he had taken a turn with
the wicked witch,
and embraced several
of her leathery demons.
He would have tumbled a munchkin
had one let him.
But one by one,
the golden bricks he stole
weighed him down. Word came
that she had found a third lover,
a shining tin man who had a good heart.

How long must they seek
before they find the wizards
of their dreams?
Some say always.
Some say it only stops
at the edge of a sea of yellow,
where they slumber forever
under the golden poppies.

This satirical look at the gung-ho unit I was once part of was inspired by John Crowe Ransom's *Captain Carpenter*. Written for Philip Levine's class, it was not published until 3 years afterwards. (It has been said, and I believe it, that Levine, Peter Everwine, Gene Bluestein and Robert Mezey—all instructors at Fresno State in the early 1960s—were responsible for more publishing poets than any college of comparable size. Herb Scott, my classmate, is an especially fine poet and widely admired. Iambic pentameter; rhyme scheme a-a-b-a.)

THE HIGH I.Q. OF WILLY WAYNE

He never was a big man, Willy Wayne,
No, he was nondescript and even plain,
But he had brawn for all his natty size,
And he could stand a nice amount of pain.

And he had visions, too. He dreamed of things
to make him big: of boots and guns and wings;
At seventeen he shrewdly realized
The army was the place for his first fling.

He joined the Paratroopers undefiled,
And soon discovered he could run three miles,
And often ran more under nightly skies,
Quietly grim, for troopers never smiled.

From private citizen to Private Wayne
Was bound to cause our hero certain pain,
But when he fell and got sand in his eyes,
He rose up manfully and ran again.

And with his training over he was led
Into a plane: the signal light was red;
But vertigo caught Willy by surprise,
He missed his jump and sat back down instead.

The colonels ranted and the captains raved,
They swore that Pvt. Willy was depraved,
And told him that regardless of his bias,
The honor of the Airborne must be saved.

His chance for glory gone, Willy, surprised,
Found chill contempt in all his buddies eyes,
And so he made a vow, brave Pvt. Wayne:
The next lift saw him off to jump again.

And he did jump: his shout was brisk and hoarse;
He struck the ground with satisfying force,
And all the troopers registered surprise
To see poor Willy where he was no more.

O, many the guess about that fatal lift,
Some said static-line, and some said drift,
But all admired the tinge of Willy's robe,
And the ribboned guts that wrapped him like a gift.

One morning in California in the early 1960s, my sister awoke, went outside — and found a 3-year-old boy face down in her swimming pool. The child was already dead, and the shock put my sister in the hospital. The baby had awakened early and wandered away from his sleeping mother, somehow opened the gate, walked to the pool's edge and apparently tried to walk on the calm, blue surface.

ELEGY FOR A DROWNED CHILD

The third year of his life
was turning when he strayed
through the sunlit gate
and fell into brightness
to become a drifting angel
forever looking downward,
thin arms spread like wings.

He made no outcry. Too young
to know what had gone wrong
with his world, he breathed
the blue softness of his
surroundings, and made
some small attempt to splash
as he had in his wading pool.

There might have been some
missing of his mother, asleep
in the early light,
but darkness came quickly,
and that at least was right.
Child, you couldn't have suffered
like those who held you dear.
May you run, breathless forever,
in the blue fields of Somewhere.

OZARK AUTUMN

It could be a blue lagoon,
this small pool on Buffalo Creek,
and the children bronze platoons
of a people who once made

arrowheads here. See the sleek
young mothers as they wade,
skirts bunched among the wild
onions; see the babies splashing

in the shallows. Swimmers watch
as the sun rests in a mountain notch
and the creek comes alive
with kids racing for one last dive.

It's Tom and Huck and Becky again,
here in these Ozark shallows,
watched by the ghosts of Indians
in the blue haze of the hollows.

AS A LAD, I SLEPT WITH MY COUSINS

As a lad, I slept with my cousins
when they came visiting from far away,
and at first we slept six to a bed,
girls and boys, feet to heads,
passing thus our youngest seasons.

Then strangely (I don't know when
it first began) our toes ran
wild to roam under quilts
as patchwork as our urges,
and giggles hid guilts.

O God my help in ages past,
where were you the night heaven
brushed me, soft as an angel's wing,
when out of my darkness came light,
and out of my silence came singing?

THE BALLAD OF THE FACTORY WORKER

Dedicated to Phillips Petroleum Company

Promptly at seven he clocks in,
goes to his post and commences
the manufacture of better living,
assembly-line love, or shoestrings,
something that takes getting used to.

But he works for a premier company,
and it's worth all the effort he gives.
Someday it will pay off handsomely,
with a plaque and a retirement party,
and a speech from his boss that's a beauty.

But should he not reach retirement,
should he fall by the wayside, rejected,
he'll have failed to out-robot the robots,
he'll have put too much faith in his spirit,
and not enough in the corporate body.

In the words of Walter P. Chrysler,
you can't keep a good company down,
not with the taxpayers behind it.
We are all so brittle and bright,
the products of modern technology.

LOBO

— *44 Poems* —

In 1940 in the high Sierra hamlet of Taylorsville, California, I was in the 2nd grade in a one-room brick school that was built in 1865 and still stands. The town was old and beautiful, with pines and mountains fringing a golden valley. A sparkling stream that once powered a mill ran through Taylorsville, and was encircled by tall cattails. Through this maze of vegetation I tunneled like a mole, to end at the edge of the little river, hidden from all eyes. There I would sit and dream, safe in my secret world, which every kid has—if only in his own imagination. This poem has been recorded and is in 35 anthologies.

THE DREAMER

He spent his childhood hours in a den
of rushes, watching the grey rain braille
the surface of the river. Concealed
from the outside world, nestled within,
he was safe from parents, God, and eyes
that look upon him accusingly,
as though to say: Even at your age,
you could do better. His camouflage
was scant but it served, and at evening,
when fireflies burned holes into heaven,
he took a path homeward in the dark,
a small Noah, leaving his safe ark.

LOBO, 1972

When I was very young, my grandmother, the mother of my mother, came to live with us in Mesa, Arizona, where dad was a handmilker on a dairy. She was a large, white haired old lady who always seemed to be seated in a rocking chair, in a white apron, shelling peas. I did not know she was even then dying of cancer. I did not know what cancer was. And then one day, Grandma was not there. Only her chair, which somehow to me embodied the splendor of her spirit as she went on with her work until the very end.

THE ROCKING CHAIR

I can still see Grandmother
shelling peas in the rocker
on a sunny day, "Another
pail," she would say, removing
her sunbonnet. I had eyes
only for the rocker, then.
Carved, ornate, how it would spin
in its small orbit, a prize
ship on a wooden ocean.
Somewhere she lies buried, now,
dead of cancer at seventy,
but on windy days I see,
or think I do, the chair rocking,
and the late sun makes shadows
of its substance on the wall.

LOBO, 1972

I had a maternal uncle named Cleve who was 35 when I knew
him. I was about 4, but Cleve himself was just 7—for he was men-
tally handicapped. I saw something Christ-like about the shambling,
gentle soul, who did only good and who was one day crucified in
part by the loss of his thumb to a hatchet. The incident really hap-
pened, and I can still hear his cries of pain, even though my uncle
has now been dead for 30 years. Notice the use of religious language
and symbols in words like "congregations of the wise" and "to live
and laugh with children."

CLEVE

How often, in the days before I knew
the design of our lives was different,
did honest Cleve, my simple-minded kin,
sacrifice dark walnuts with a hatchet
and offer the flesh to me, a nephew
too young to know he wasn't a real child.
And then one day the bright, deceptive axe
turned his hand and severed his holding thumb,
which kicked in the grass like a thick, red, worm,
torn from its roots by some descending beak.
Decades have since dissolved like winter breath,
but still I think of him whose curious birth
left him barred from all the congregations
of the wise, to live and laugh with children.

My family were sharecroppers and migrant cottonpickers through much of my youth. We picked cotton, hoed corn, and cut broomcorn all over the south but especially in Texas, Oklahoma, Arizona and California. Way back when, cotton fields had a tree or two left standing. These were called "weighing trees," because the weighing scales hung from the main limb by a chain. In my day, scales mostly hung from a tripod of two-by-fours. This poem is about the labor of cottonpicking, in the broiling Texas sun. Again, the poet uses heavy religious symbolism relating to the crown of thorns, the endless trek to the crucifixion, the suffering and pain. It is a short epic of human suffering—which picking cotton certainly was to me. The form is that of a sonnet, iambic pentameter.

THE WEIGHING-TREE

Here, my father said, is another field.
It stalks were fuller than the ones we'd left
not many days before, and each would yield
all we might ask of it. Indeed, the drift
of those white rows of dark, clawed burrs of cotton
I can see still, and feel their curving thorns
piercing my hands. What should have been forgotten
only recalls the bending, and my brow burns
from the stiff twigs that hid the last low boll.
There was no end to it. My father's goal
was never mine, and yet I could not see
beyond the end of rows that had no end,
except to see the laddered wagon-stand,
and hang my load upon the weighing-tree.

One hot summer day in California where I briefly managed a small ranch for a rich man, a friend and I began a "back burn" to stave off the danger of a grass fire burning the house down. In a simple human maneuver against nature, meaning no harm, we saw a tiny tragedy we had caused.

THE BURNING

East of the shed, the yellow sawgrass
explodes from earth, a bright confusion
made brighter by the sun. The last rain
fell last year, and summer is on us.

With one neighbor and a garden hose,
The cautious work begins: a small flame
first, then a bright and noisy mowing
that startles the scissortails.

who wheel above the flowing smoke
as though playing a game. Soon
the pasture, black under the sun,
holds a last few dying embers.

Then from the field a burning mouse
drags blindly toward the shed,
and a safety it remembers.

This poem rhymes in loose fashion and is loosely syllabic in construction. Crows were once the embodiment of hell's evil to grain farmers who often "mined" their roosts and blew them to kingdom come. Note the flight sequences, as of batlike creatures or even warplanes, foreshadowing the "war" to come.

THE CROW KILL

The day the wheat was ready,
dark forms fell like rain.
From high on their struts of wind
the whirling raiders came.

to mutilate and shatter
the bronze ranks of grain.
We saw our hopes smothered
by a fungus of wings.

The blackness disappeared
with dusk, but long after
their deadly work was done,
we heard their harsh laughter,

and saw sluggish pinions
hauling them to their orchard lair,
sooty children of the devil
with souls of slag.

We let them brag.
We let them stir the leaves
as they settled on dynamite
we'd planted. Cued by wires

and prima-cord, each blast
would make limbs shrapnel,
until the roosting forms,
lit by our man-made dawn,

mulched with blood and bone
their nesting ground. Spies
return. The orchard sprouts crows
like fat, black plums.

The plunger falls. Current
flails the wires. The night tears
like rotten canvas, and in soft,
wet whispers, a dark rain falls.

Trapping is still a part of life in the Ozarks, where I now live. The first trapper I ever knew was an old black man in the Oklahoma hills who lived in a reeking "holler" where the side of his barn was covered with raw, yellow hides tacked tightly on boards and drying in the sun. Like much of my work, this poem is also a "statement" about the hard life of the artists (in any medium) who try for the rich prizes-but don't quit when they lose. Free verse.

THE TRAPPER

He follows the line northeast,
past the Ludlow cabin, the dry creeks,
the weedgrown furrows that still twist
like crooked limbs through dead fields.
Only the muskrats live here now,
making blind forays against his traps.

Old Ludlow said once, "Try for fox;
something that'll increase the value
of your traps. There's shine to muskrat
pelts, but there ain't no money in 'em."
And so it is that every season,
he tries for the rich prize, and losing

does not make him want it less. He covets
what is hard to come by, skins his lean catch,
and tacks it up to dry, leaving his traps
baited and open. In a furrow
by the shack he has seen fresh spoor,
and knows he will come back tomorrow.

PUBLISHED SOMEWHERE, long ago, I forget where.

Tractor accidents have always been common on the farm, and
when I was a teenager in Oklahoma, this was one, in which an old
man lost his youngest son. Although I'm not religious I love biblical
imagery and often utilize some of the parables in my poems. It's also
possible to see how man is humbled and crushed by another form
of "god"—the machine. Some rhyme, 7-syllable syllabics.

BENJAMIN

You are dead now Benjamin.
The fields you worked lie fallow
in the sun. Last year's corn
stiffens in the winter's wind,
and the pasture oaks relive
their yearly dying. By the barn
the ice thickens in the trough,
and cattle stray in the slough
near where you died. Pinned beneath
the old tractor you plowed with,
torn by its lugs, you could not shout
or know when we dug you out.
My 75th winter
will bring no celebration.
Ice cracks under my feet
like fishbones in the dry creeks
of summer. In my cabin
the light burns low, my son,
and soon I must sleep.

Published somewhere . . .

Nothing exceptional here—just a different kind of "Currier and Ives" illustration. Some rhyme and off-rhyme.

CURRIER & IVES

The winter sky
is like an old man's face,
the water in the pond
like faded overalls.

Southbound geese
tow their wake
behind them,
and fences take

crooked steps in snow.
Beyond the red barn,
the day begins to die.
Clouds strangle on a hill,

the hours end
in a furnace glow,
the evening comes on
like cold, grey bones.

THE LONG MARCH

Jimmy Jones was a paratrooper buddy who "tagged" on for an extra jump shortly before going on his honeymoon. His parachute never opened and he smashed so hard into the earth he bounced like a giant rag doll. He didn't have to make the jump. He did so out of pride. Pride does indeed go before a fall. The "glass eye" reflecting a soldier's nightmare was the camera of the military photographer, whose job was to photograph all military tragedies.

FOR A DEAD PARATROOPER

Memento mori in shades of grey
adorn my album, as he adorned
the earth that October day when,
out of an aircraft, he took the
giant step. Kentucky bluegrass
was marred by patriot colors of
white and red, and troopers ringed
his hammered body, brutally curious

of the dead. In the photo, he
sprawls like a puppet cut from
its strings; stiffened fingers
locked in the D-ring in death as
they were in life. I remember his
face as he fell, and wonder what
his final understanding was like.

It's strange to look back on those
accidents that composed my living,
each caught in a glass eye that
reflected some soldier's nightmare.
Jones, decades have passed and so
have you. Your picture crumbles,
but it's all I have. The years bring
rot to both the living and the dead.

HARPERS, 1966

    As I sailed out under the Golden Gate bound for Harry Truman's
"police action," I was struck by the strange anomaly of killers and
thugs being saved from a combat death by being behind bars, while
law abiding citizen went forth to kill and die with the blessings of
their nation. Years later I would write about something similar. A
rapist in the prison hospital (Springfield, Missouri) lay sullenly re-
ceiving kidney dialysis—a life saving treatment that I could not
begin to afford for my own children. Yet a rapist and murderer was
getting it free—and taxpayers were paying for it.

KOREA BOUND, 1952

Braced against the rise and fall of the ocean,
holding the rail, we listen to the shrill
complaining of the waves against the hull,
and see the Golden Gate rise with our motion.
Some hours previous, bearing duffels
as heavy as our thoughts, we would onward
like slaves in some gigantic pyramid,
selected by our Pharoah for burial
against our wills. Now we watch Alcatraz
sink into the water, and visualize
the pale, amorphous masks of prisoners,
whose lack of freedom guarantees their lives.

Then my first son, Christopher Brandon Childress, was born April 6, 1967, while I was an MFA student at the University of Iowa, my mind was still on war—and America was still in one. I wrote this poem because, in a futile and frightening sense, all our babies are born to the terrible possibilities of dying in some war created by politicians for reasons of power, or madness, or both.

FOR MY FIRST SON

Shadows of trenchcoats darken
his crib, tiny fingers grope
towards a future of steel
cables on a ship's deck,
weighted duffel, and arms
that drag him downward.

His small skull is bound
in iron confinement, the
doll's face pressed
to his mother's breast
darkens like crisped leather

in a flamethrower's blast.
I see trenchfoot and worms,
wounds spilling gangrene,
his delicate skin torn
by shrapnel. And then,

with eyes empty as spent
cartridges, he is packaged
for home. For these are the
gifts of male birthdays,
wrapped in patriot slogans,
and sent by lying leaders.

Happy birthday to you,
Happy birthday to you,
Happy birthday my son,
Happy birthday to you.

LOBO, book, 1972

This is a poem that is, quite simply, about war—real war, not the
kind "fought" by movie actors with fake sets and fake guns. My war
contained limbs of little children, blown away by 155mm howitzers
and mortars. A child is a child, regardless of nationality.

THE LONG MARCH

North from Pusan,
trailing nooses of dust,
we dumbly followed
leaders whose careers
hung on victory.

The road might
have been the Appian Way
except for the
starved children lining it.
We gave what we could

to hold back the grave,
but in Pusan the dead-truck
snuffled through frozen dawns
retrieving bones in thin sacks,
kids who would never beg again.

When we bivouacked
near Pyongtaek, a soldier
fished a bent brown stick
from a puddle. It was
the arm of someone's child.

Not far away, the General
camps with his press corps.
Any victory will be his
for us, there is only
the long march to Viet Nam.

One of the most terrible sights any GI must become used to is the sight of starving children. Giving them rations (as many GIs did against orders) merely staved off the inevitable. In this poem a simple farm boy weeps inwardly while thinking of how little it would take to make everything right again with these kids. This could be Latin America or Afghanistan.

LETTER HOME

Mother, they line the roads
like broken stalks,
children with bellies swollen,
and O, the flowers
of their faces, petals all torn,
and the flags
of their threadbare garments.
Mother, we give
them everything in our packs
and still they moan
so sadly More with eyes
like stone.
These kids will never sing
again.
O, mother, wish me home!
With just one field of Kansas grain,
what I can do for them.

This poem was written with Douglas MacArthur firmly in mind. His men once called him "Dugout Doug", and it always amused me to see him wading ashore in some "combat zone"—while a PR-man landed first with movie cameras. All my buddies were delighted when Truman fired MacArthur. In a larger sense, it is about the executives of war who send the corporate bodies in to be made into confetti.

COMBAT IAMBIC

Once in a distant war which was no war,
mired in the unclean paddies, bleeding clean
my buddies died while tracer bullets tore
through earth and armored vests like acetylene.
Our General, in rearmost echelon,
with fancy unfired pistol near his thigh,
barked militant commands and acted out
his manly role untouched by fire. O, sir,
I pray Beelzebub, Lord of the Flies,
to rear his maggot children in your eyes,
where curled like living lashes they can give
the atmosphere that suits a General's mind.

This poem takes us into the mind of a victim of battle fatigue, whose sight of a soldier's shattered arm falling to earth tips him into momentary madness, and sends him behind the green walls of a military hospital. Such a man George S. Patton slapped during WW2. But G.S. Patton never spent days and nights by the hundreds in freezing snow and cold rain—while being in constant hazard of death. If he had been, Patton might have buckled, too. Many generals never see real combat.

SHELLSHOCK

I am MacFatridge as he was then,
torn by the mine he was defusing;
at the aid-tent door his arm fell off,
and a Medic stooped to retrieve it
and stood as though lugging a melon
that had burst in the sun.

There are those of us who are not tough
despite all they told us. If I cry
now, no one seems to care, but before,
I would have been punished with a laugh.
I wish that underneath the green sky
of this room, images of terror
would come again: that the emerald door
I can't pass would let me out to sleep.

LOBO, book, 1972

   This macabre little poem speaks for itself. It could fit any number
of top brass. This is not to say all generals are useless, or just in a
war to advance their careers. General Maxwell D. Taylor was greatly
respected by his men, as was "Ike" Eisenhower and certain others.
My favorite is the general, now dead, who managed to get a Silver
Star without getting a Purple Heart. Pretty lucky.

DEATH OF A GENERAL

At the autopsy, the knife
inflicted the first real wound
his body had ever known.
The incision, deep and clean,
revealed a petrified heart,
and lungs unpowderstained.

He was survived by a wife,
who informed the reporters,
crisply, of his lifelong goal.
He had missed it by one war.
We probed for, but never found,
any evidence of a soul.

He was famed for discipline,
and we saw why. In a corner
of his stomach, well-hidden,
we found a thick volume
of military law.
No one was chief mourner

at his funeral. The guns
for the salute were pointed
at him. He was anointed
by a cloudburst, but his sins
remained. The medals on his chest
caught the light like cartridge-brass.

When I wrote this sonnet I was corresponding with a young marine at Khe Sanh. I remember that he was a good writer, and had sent some material to a magazine I was then publishing. We became good friends by mail. The last I heard of him was when Khe Sanh came under massive attack and the marines abandoned it. I've always hoped he got home all right.

THE WAR LESSON

After they taught us guns, they showed us how
to throw grenades. We watched the meadows grow
momentarily large, then settle down
in bits of pummeled earth, and every man
saw it as the disrupted flesh of those
we were hired to kill. It was a game
we wished might end, but no, we had to fight
as they would fight, our goals beyond our sights.

At Khe Sanh, when the mortar rounds had hushed
and we moved out, I saw upon a bush
the burned and dangling genitals of a Cong.
Or did I see? We moved as in a dream,
a dream that paced our lives to marching songs,
and bundled flaming children in their screams.

THE FAR POINT MAGAZINE, Canada, 1969

Viet Nam was America's first living-room war, thanks to the Pandora's Box begun by Philo T. Farnsworth in the 1920's. I wish most naively, that "TV" had never been invented. It is now our most insidious drug, claiming about half the lives of our children with dumb, dead language and hardening them against the horrors of war. Loosely, iambic pentameter with on-again off-again rhyme schemes.

THE VIEWER

Saturday brings the weekend roundup news:
My television tube serves up a child
done to a turn, small peasant under glass.
Great men prepare their wisdom for the world,
eyeing the camera's eye, casting their pearls.
I smile at talk of peace or words of war,
and laugh when corporate businessmen endow

with burning profits some deserving college.
It's little enough to pay for patronage.
Chamber of Commerce spiels delight my ear,
and Legionnaires snarl like *Sturmabteiling*.
Speeches are made by Kiwanis and Lions
as to who has done the most in these odd times.
Sophia Loren's lips are called "bee-stung."
John Waynes loses a cancerous left lung.

I turn the dial: the child returns again,
this time in glowing color, with raw, red skin.
Huntley and Brinkley comment, solemn, wise,
two kind and well-paid men. (How soon my eyes
adjust from grey to red. It almost seems
I'm there, hearing that burnt child scream.)
Jackie Kennedy is one of the best-dressed ten.
Millions in India starve for lack of grain.

I turn the dial: the President, the Pope
prepare to speak, to bring us viewers hope.
The President reaffirms our stand abroad.
The Pope is vaguer, and says Trust in God.
But now the news is over. Channel Nine
comes on to tell me that It's Raleigh Time!
I wonder if their free coupons will buy
copper enough to weight a dead child's eyes.

I was teaching at an Illinois college when I wrote this poem. Hawks sucked up beer in American Legion Halls and "fought" their old wars while jeering us liberals who were antiwar. The peach symbol was dubbed, "Track of the American Chicken." Many legionnaires could not understand how an exparatrooper with three honorable discharges—myself—could be so antiwar. But I knew.

MIDWEST LEGION BAR

They hunch in denimed rows,
beering it up in workmen's clothes,
running to fat now, getting old.
Behind the veterans faces
lie other faces, puzzled, lost,

wondering where the last
great war, the one that really counted,
went-wondering how kids today
can pervert all the dreams
all of them fought for,

the flag, football, boy scout hikes.
Now they stubbornly pit emotion
against younger, wiser men,
curse them for not knowing America's needs,
and go back to joking about niggers and kikes.

LOBO, book, 1972

My first dead soldier; a buddy in the combat engineers who
caught fire while fueling his hot 'dozer; an amazing night-landing by
flashlight by a heroic helicopter pilot—these were the people I
never really knew in Korea.

TRYING TO REMEMBER PEOPLE
I NEVER REALLY KNEW

There was that guy
on that hill in Korea.
Exploding gasoline made him
a thousand candles bright.
We guided the Samaritan copter
in by flashlight
to a rookery of rocks,
a huge, fluttering nightbird
aiming at darting fireflies,
and one great firefly
rolling in charred black screams.

There was the R.O.K. soldier
lying in the paddy,
his lifted arms curved
as he stiffly embraced death,
a tiny dark tunnel over his heart.
Such a small door
for something as large as life
to escape through.

Later. between pages and chapters
of wars not yet written up
in Field Manuals or Orders of the Day,
there came shrieking down
from a blue Kentucky sky
a young paratrooper whom technology failed.
(I must correct two common errors:
they are never called *shroud lines*,
and paratroopers do not cry *Geronimo*.)

I wish I could say
that all three men fathered sons,
that some part of them still lived.
But maybe I don't, for the children's ages
would now be such as to make them
ready for training as hunters of men,
to stalk dark forests
where leaden rains fall with a precision
that can quench a hunter's fire.

THE CONDEMNED

There is something chilling about the little wars that constantly go on in nature because in them we can see ourselves and "our larvae." Free verse. A long-time favorite of mine that, to me at least, is aging well. Written mid-1960s.

THE CONFLICT

There were two sovereigns
in a shed, a wasp
who built castles of mud
and a spider whose throneroom
shivered with trophies.

They spied each other.
The wasp drummed his wings
and danced, the spider
readied venom. One day
at dusty noon, their aims

coalesced: a dark lance
fell, and spider and wasp
were united in a union
only death could undo.
How strange to see two rulers

so proximal, so wedded in
the turmoil of undeclared war
and insect politics.
But we know such tricks
ourselves, and pass them on
to our larvae.

LOBO, book, 1972

In 1965 I was a counselor at San Francisco Juvenile Hall, reporting for work very early each morning. One morning I saw, to my astonishment, a salamander crawling along in a gutter after a brief rain. Salamanders are sometimes picked up and dropped by rain clouds but I have never seen one in a city before, and using both myth and reality, flew away to fantasyland. Nine-syllable syllabic lines, off-rhyme.

THE SALAMANDER

Older than Methuselah's conception,
his blank eyes watch the socketed stars
go out as dawn extinguishes them.
For him darkness is the only light,
and he sees in the shadows what mankind
does in the sun. A water-sweeper
swirls the dregs of yesterday's used hours
into the gutters. He fronts the tide,
moving with it under the sweeper's,
under the streets transiently clean.
Legend alone knows his destination,
and it has said he lives in the fires
that gnaw the edge of the underworld,
just north of God, just south of Satan.

This is about Adam and Eve, and Sin, and The Garden, and other Unmentionables. The last few lines are especially revelatory of "the beast within." Some rhyme, seven-syllable syllabic lines.

THE FLIGHT

It was after the bright fruit
had been eaten, after the gate
opened like a cave before them
that they fled, and in pursuit
were the very beasts who slept
at their feet before. They kept
only to the narrow path,
for on the other, thorns grew.

They couldn't escape the likeness
of the place. There were flowers
everywhere, of the kind they
had been told grew only within.
Nor could they hesitate,
for now he possessed powers
no man had known, and always,
the animals kept pace.

Night gathered and it was new,
for they had known no night
in the garden. In a lair
of vines and tendrils they made
their bed, and in the darkness
found what they had fled to find,
only to see the great beasts leap,
their gleaming claws bared.

In 1965 in San Francisco, a "cutter" was on the loose. He had slashed several women, and I continually warned my own wife never to drive with her car doors unlocked. He was likened to a modern-day Jack the Ripper, and that is how I saw him. He wasn't caught. He's still out there somewhere, with his scalpel, his razor, or his knife. Perhaps he is the original Jack the Ripper. Perhaps he will never die.

JACK THE RIPPER

Drifting through evening's hemorrhage,
did he blink at the gas-lamp like
the night creature he was? Darkness
was his country, and a dark urge
drove him to lurk in shadows
and in parks for the strident girls,

who waited for anyone but him. Stare
met stare. Their widening eyes
meant comprehension, a picture
on a page, a body that closed
a gutter like gate,
a bloodstained knife and no suspect.

His fingers opened each drama,
and he relished the Aceldama
of their making, knowing morning
would open on a relative or lover
with no opposite, whose eyes
would wake to recognize and fear.

Murderers leave their work
like reapers leave each severed
golden stalk, for others to bind
and cure. Officials bay with civic
mouths for psychopaths; police
claim suspects, and no one is sure.

In the cotton fields I worked as a child, I played with any kid I could find, and was glad for the company. But mostly we worked, all races, creeds and colors. I knew of, but didn't understand, the hostility between grown men of different races—and true bigotry isn't restricted to any one race. Years later a pancake company, fearful of a marketing backlash, began changing the "Aunt Jemina" image to a more updated version. This poem, free verse satire, grew from that. This poem has been anthologized.

THE METAMORPHOSIS OF AUNT JEMIMA

For years she smiled
with her apron white teeth,
a honeydew grin
warming the kitchen of whitefolks' homes

Her face was mellow brown,
because black was not yet beautiful,
and under a knotted kerchief
her hair was frizzed and crisp

and something kids marveled at.
Sometimes, after a Steppin Fetchit movie,
Aunt Jemima minded a hot stove,
always smiling,
that we might taste a simpler age.

But I grew up, and had children
and breakfasts of my own,
and one day the portrait on the box
was not the same.
The smile was thinner and colder

and the eyes frightened my pale offspring.
Still, I brought her home,
for old habits die hard.
And how better could I reward
all her loyalty and kindness?

It's too late to help her now, of course.
I only wish I could have foreseen
the dark, congested face,
the upraised hand,
the fist clenched against all
the white tomorrows,
the death of pancakes in America.

AMERICA MAGAZINE, 1969; BELLY OF THE SHARK
(Anthology) 1972

Eighteen years ago on a freelance assignment I visited Dickson
Mounds, Illinois, and wrote a magazine story about the place. I love
history and archaeology, and this ancient grave site transported
me back through the centuries to stand beside a woman in the first
agonies of birth — and the final agony of death.

FOR AN INDIAN WOMAN
DEAD IN CHILDBIRTH

Death stopped your
attempt at life long
before Columbus came,
and took you from your
mud hut to lie in state
before these gawking
strangers. Fibers
of flesh still halo
the loins that grip
the tiny warrior
who wouldn't leave you.
His thin ivory
wrists grope toward
a life that never came.
I think of the shamans,
whose witchcraft
failed to unclench
your pelvis.
You could not give
what would not be given.
I watch the gaping
tourists who, with
kodaks ready, picture
your pain, and mother,
I am in pain and I
am your son, centuries
late, transcribing
your passing.

We think of addiction as being a "new" problem, but it has always been with us—at least in the form of our oldest drug, alcohol, which is also our worst. In the 19th century heroin and opium were legal, and gifts to friends were often goldplated hypodermics. Genesis 9:20 speaks of the first alcoholic, Noah, drunk and naked in his tent. Various Indians use narcotics as religious dream agents. This poem is about a heroin addict—a college friend of mine who, to the bitter end, insisted he could control his habit.

THE ADDICT

From the steel window, stained with the dust
of aumumn winds, he watches the night
peel from the sky like dead skin. The season
turns pastures to rust and brings no heat,
and under his feet, the stone floor is cold.

Some have said a longing of the mind
keeps him alive, and eases his pain
by settling with a delicate rain
the thin dust of his dreams. At the edge
of his illusionary world

soft walls keep him from harm. God insists
that this be so, and in his green gown,
pads though secret porticoes and halls,
and brings a shining needle, and is kind.

The child described in this poem remains my most searing memory of juvenile counselor days. If he is alive, and I hope he is, he's now 26—because he was actually five when I knew him. His worthless parents had given him up and I still see him, and will always see him as the small, forlorn little boy trying to act tough among kids thrice his size. I used to look into his locked cell at night, where he lay in restless sleep, sometimes crying out—and I wanted with all my heart to take his parents out and drown them in San Francisco Bay. Unfortunately, scum floats.

FOR AN 8-YEAR-OLD DELINQUENT IN JUVENILE HALL

There is no child anymore
in your eyes, although sometimes
your gestures are those of one,
and always, the voice reminds.
It's hard not to see in you
my own non-existent son.

You stand among some forty
others, dressed in the plain blue
uniform that turns all of you
into a blank human wall,
yet you stand out by virtue
of being the most small.

Now, confined in this place,
each day is just a copy
of yesterday. Your puppy
was yours to kill and dissect;
why did each bloody piece
upset the large world so?

LOBO, book, 1972

There have been many race riots in American History. Here is one event from one that took place some years ago in our nation's capitol during the Viet Nam era. Perhaps ironically, the medium is free verse.

84

COLOR

Once in Cherry
Blossom time
I saw a white
cop hit a Black
man, his brown
stick rising
and falling
like a baton
for unseen
musicians. The
blood ran red
as cherry juice,
red as the sticky
maraschino
leeched from the
red red fruit
by the mysterious
process that
rule over
cherries and men.

Shark attacks off the California coast have happened more than once. I wrote this poem around a newspaper account of one, comparing the terrible fury of a shark's ripping attack to the awesome force of a summer storm. Free verse.

THE DIVERS

We struck west toward
Catalina, past the green
seaweed beds that drowned the
grey coastline behind us.
Clouds shadowed the boat
while we, suited for survival
out of our element,
watched the sea for abalone.

Turk dove first.
I saw his body divide
the haze of plankton and
drift in a green twilight,
and that was all.
No sooner had he gone
than he was gone. Something
hit him at twenty feet, bent

in a bony arc to strike
again, and it was Turk's
own screams filling my mask.
A storm in the water, brown
cumulus forming, and bits
of Turk's suit churned upward
like yellow leaves in
the wake of my fear.

I always loved the poetry of Weldon Kees, who died long before I
ever thought of writing poetry. Like me, he also used a camera—and
used it well. I was into dramatic sonnets (this poem was written in
class), and this one is rather sonorous. But it's heartfelt. Generally
iambic pentameter.

FOR WELDON KEES

From the dark span that saw his own span break,
he once looked westward over raining hills,
and saw in asphalt caves the things that killed
themselves and him. The treadmill of his thoughts
turned in the empty rooms where telephones
demanded Robinson, but Robinson
was never anywhere he ought to be.
Later, in the mock-up of a city,
a man was seen: the man was Robinson.
But no one ever knew what route he took,
and no one ever knew if he was dead.
None of it mattered. A few pages hold
the words of him who found the world too cold,
and left it, leaving all he said unsaid.

THE CABALIST

LOBO, book, 1972

I wrote most of the following poems while an editor/writer at National Geographic Magazine in Washington DC in 1970. Washington sent me into a bleakness tailspin, and for my year there I wrote some crazy stuff. Maybe it kept me from becoming a genuine crazy. I was also in my 30's, and convinced that my life was a hollow drum that the establishment was banging on as hard as possible.

THE CABALIST

At 36, he has an education,
a job, good prospects
for the future,
yet he looks for any reason
to cancel all his contracts,
to somehow ease
his rioting nerves and brain.

He studies the occult,
tries everything astral,
consults signs, omens, charts,
all the mystic arts
that seem to work for others.

O, surely such mysteries will make him pure!
From the Region of the Sun
he will call back power.
His strength will intensify
in the Region of the Moon.
In the Pose of an Adept
he will meditate;
he will assume the Star Pose,
the poses of Peacock and Raven.

And finally he will enter
the monastery of his mind,
shutting out the strident city
and the world.
But for all his focusing of power,
he knows he must be devious.
He was born under the sign of Aquarius,
and hears the waters rising
hour by hour.

This poem appeared in some magazine, I forget where. Actually, it's little more than an old medieval formula for black magic, placed into loose *vers libre*. Try it for Halloween.

THE HAND OF GLORY

Take the right hand
of a felon
who is hanging
from a gibbet
by the king's highway.
Wrap it in part
of a funeral pall,
and so wrapped,
squeeze it well.

Put it into
an earthen vessel
with zimat, nitre,
salt and longpeppers,
the whole well powdered.

Leave it for
a fortnight, then
expose it to the sun
during the dog days only
until it becomes
quite dry.

Make a kind of candle
with the fat
of a gibbeted felon,
and virgin's wax,
sesame, horse dung,
and pony.

Then use the Hand of Glory
to hold this lighted
candle, and let this
baneful instrument
precede you everywhere you go,
and all who see it
will be paralyzed forever.

Published in some long-since-lost magazine, and in LOBO. Spain is always a trip back in time, and as a paratrooper on leave there in the late 1950s, I reveled in the history glowing from museum shadows. The Prado still remains one of my great memories of Europe.

MUSEO DEL PRADO

Over these dim walls Weyden's genius broods,
his dark religiousness forever frozen
in scabs of pigment on a skin of cloth.
I see the symbols of mad Goya's wrath,
each bloody sketch, each pattern of confusion,
and watch a painted Christ feed multitudes.

The dimness masks the brilliance of the minds
that gave such celebration to these halls,
and in the shadows, Goya's leering fiends
mean more to me than Brueghal's pastorals.
I watch the way his twisted demons run,
and gaze at *Jupiter Devouring His son.*

The corridors are silent in the Prado,
with the kind of silence that imparts
force to the lean lines of a *bastinado*
held by a Christian hand. The cruel arts
of the *corrida* hang in the galleries,
and rotting corpses hang from painted trees.

Vampirism fascinates me. There are people who truly believe they are vampires (or even werewolves), and since it's no fun being a writer if you can't "become" something, I decided to be a vampire for awhile. Some off-rhyme, some rhyme, free verse.

VAMPIRE

Always it was my shadow.
It had ways of leaving
without asking leave,
and always, grieving
was sure to follow. Someone
would grieve a woman

I'd never heard of, and reveal
her sad fate to others.
And each night, something killed;
something frightful and dark stalked
the city, and no one dared
to ask about its diet.

I did all I could. Nothing.
The things my shadow did weren't mine.
(Yet I've been finding stains
on shirts I know I've worn,
and why memories of screams
slowing pooling in my mind?)

They cornered it at last,
tracked it to this old house
and to a kind of dusty chest.
I was proud as anyone
to see them poise a wooden fang
and drive it home, bit by bit,

and though I felt no sympathy,
the devil knows I felt pain.
But all that was months ago.
Now I sit inside, listening to rain
lamenting, and to the dry rustle
of my shadow, growing like a tail.

When I was a country kid who often walked home from plowing Oklahoma red dirt after dark, I always dreaded crossing an old oak-planked bridge by a dark slough. I never once walked across that bridge, nor did I run. I flew across that bridge. My feet never touched its planks. Because under that bridge lurked trolls—and trolls loved to feast on little kids. Free verse, fantasy.

HUNTING THE TROLLS

When I was young, I believed in trolls
and looked for them under moss-planked bridges
and in secret orchards late at night,
where yellow fruit glowed like eyes
in the hanging moonlight.

Come deeper, deeper
whispered the orchard trees,
until I lost myself in a maze
of shadows, where vines hung like leathery arms,
bearing fruit no animal would eat.

Years closed behind me like latches
as I prowled abandoned barns
and searched old houses with gables like tusks.
Already I half knew what I would find,
but never when or where.

I prowled the banks of Devil's Slough
where rushes clicked in the cold wind,
and always, always, I grew closer
to some thick shape, looming just out of sight.

Come deeper, deeper
murmured the dark water, the unreal orchards,
and finally I walked on naked bone,
leaving behind in my hoofed tracks
only a dark unholy image
for the morning sun
to cower from.

In 1969 I was teaching at an Illinois college and lived in an old 19th century country house—a real firetrap. I finished my first novel there, and fearful it might burn up, took it to my office in the red brick English Department building. On New Year's Eve the building caught fire and burned up, taking my novel and all carbons. I just know it would've been a best seller. This poem is about a bat that got loose from the attic and scared my wife half to death.

THE WARLOCK

In his Edgar Poe house,
in a secret place,
he keeps the shapes
he conjures. The room holds
demons he can't hold,
and turns none loose.

Yet last night he dreamed
soft shuddering wings
and woke to find them real.
A furry demon
attacked his lamp and him.
He killed it with a broom.

Omens are only omens
and dreams just dreams,
but now he wonders
at the room above the stairs,
and studies his ancient book,
afraid to look.

Magicians, too, wait
days tomorrow
may be, bringing a sun to melt
curses deeper than marrow.
He brews what he has to brew.
The days pass like hearses.

LOBO, book, 1972

This is a very strange poem that I wrote when I was in a very
strange mood. In a way, it's almost funny. But I dare you to read it
late at night, then go to your window and hunker down and look
out to a spot just below your window...

THE WEREWOLF

There is a darkness deeper
than the far moon's unlit side,
than trees with crooked limbs,
or roots springing from shadows.

There is a furry quality to the night
and moonbeams like sharp, canine teeth
and two eyes that defy analogy.

Nothing is wrong with me. I am healthy.

There is a noise that is not the wind
in the trees, but an urgent cry
for blood. (Is it the wind in the branches
that whines so for blood?)

Nothing is wrong with me. I am healthy.

Oh, a few scattered dreams
tax even my credulity
as evening slinks forth,
and in them I lope with a howling wind

to slouch through your garden,
or lurk in the bushes lining your path,
or light your windows with my eyes.

And the wild grass of midnight
strafes my toes.

LOBO, book, 1972

In terms of form, this is an easy poem, basically trochaic tetra-
meter, with obvious rhyme scheme. Here again I'm enamored of
"personification," and I become the things talked about. I also see
trolls as the embodiment of evil—but there is a greater, far deeper
evil, and that is the beast that lurks in all of us, waiting to break free,
hiding under the bridge of our souls.

THE GOAT AND THE TROLL

Once I wandered in a dream
to a bridge that spanned a gorge.
A goat stood looking at the bridge;
underneath it crouched a troll.

Earlier, I had dreamed of horns;
cloven footprints marked my strolls.
I vowed I'd walk upon the bridge;
I vowed I'd overcome the trolls.

Now the bridge's mossy planks
echo to our goatish tread:
trolls rise howling rank on rank
which of us will end up dead?

The answer comes in horrid growls
as rage meets rage above the moat:
blood runs free from goat and devil,
goat and troll, troll and goat.

For hours they fight. The crystal stream
runs crimson froth as thick as oil.
No matter who dies, goat or troll,
in every death it's I who scream.

Yesterday, I killed a dog.
Now I seek a child to rape.
For I am both Gog and Magog.
Goat and troll. There's no escape.

This poem appeared nowhere. Odd as it may sound, I was trying to think of a way to pay some small tribute to my long-time friend, publisher E. V. Griffith of *Poetry Now*. He once published a poetry magazine called *HEARSE*, and that's how this quaint effort began.

THE HEARSES

The hearses are passing my door,
long and black
with their drivers
all in black inside them.
One beckons to me.
"Come ride with us," he says.

Someone is at my side,
my mother, my father, someone.
They pull me away
from the door, and I am told,
"You have been a bad boy.
Bad boys do not get to ride in hearses."

O, I am saddened and the tears come.
I can see in my mind
the interior of those hearses,
all silk and velvet, and I weep.
I weep but the hearses keep passing.

Soon they will be gone,
but I know what I must do.
"I have been bad," I call out.
"I cannot ride with you today."
The man only smiles and says,
"Do not worry, child.
We will pass this way again."

I've always been partial to this poem, which appears in the last issue of Hearse. It was written when I was 37, the "noon" of my life. I love the language, the "corridors of glass" (hourglass), the "dusty hours" (sands of time), the commonality of death for both the high and the low. Roughly iambic trimeter with good off rhyme. Christ is the only non-rhyme, but is could slant-rhyme with "glass" and "grace".

SPAN

My sun is poised at noon,
relentless to begin
its final arc.
Winds are eroding me
that blinded Cleopatra
and gave Anthony to the dark.

The dusty hours flow
through corridors of glass
that ushered Tutankhamen
and framed Pavlova's grace.
With dancer and with Pharoah,
I share all we hold common.

I sink into the sands
that smothered mighty Caesar;
that packed the tomb of Christ
and measured Mary's bed.
Each day the span decreases
from the living to the dead.

How this poem cam about:

I had an aunt, crippled on her right side by polio, but amazingly versatile with her one useful hand and leg. She dragged one side, had an angular, witchlike face (and sometimes a temper to match). She smoked a corncob pipe, and looked—to us urchins—like we thought a witch should. We called her Aunt Sam, and often teased her dozen or so cats, but in our way we loved her. She died in her seventies years ago, but I still remember picking cotton alongside her in Oklahoma. The first line of the poem, the "witch's incantation," came from her attempts to speak Spanish. It was years before I knew what it meant—"Vamos a la casa, poca tiempo!—Her way of saying "Get to the house right now!" The poem is in *Vers Libre.*

THE SORCERESS

Boma stela casa poca timbo
My aunt said, and green corn grew
where she placed her withered feet.
Others thought she was old and crazy.

But I knew she was a witch from the start.
I was fascinated by her gift of tongues.
She talked to roots and berries by the hours,
and they sang back to her.

By the barn one summer day,
She fell down and started kicking. "Another
fit," my father grunted—but I had seen
her earlier, communing with spiders,
and I knew she was just casting a spell.

One night the sky grew shimmering trees
and deep voices split the dark.
Cyclones touched down, hundreds died,
but we were safe. "Thank God", my mother said,
Little knowing she had a sorceress to thank.

Years went away and I left for war
with the forces of evil. She gave me an amulet
to keep me from harm, an enchanted diamond
mined from a broken fruit jar.

When I returned
I found her in a tin shack, thinboned
and tallowy, dying with no one
to admire her magic.

That night I sat beside her as she slept,
her seamed face softened by candlelight,
and at midnight ten thousand stately spiders
came down and wrapped her in gauze,
and carried her webbed spirit away.

UNPUBLISHED POEM, as far as I can remember.

When I was an undergraduate caring for a small California cattle ranch for a rich man who paid slave wages, flies attracted by cattle were a common problem. The cattle were sprayed against them, and apparently one of the affected flies made it as far as my kitchen sink before flipping over and beginning its death-buzz. The buzz, however, attracted a spider, and I turned back just in time to see the spider scuttling up a gossamer strand with the fly in its mouth. The poem started out to be an iambic pentameter sonnet, but came up one line too many — 15.

THE FLY

I watched a crippled fly as it lay dying
on my sink's edge, in delicate counterpoise
between life and death, thrusting up its feet
in mute protest towards the firmament,
No sound told me it knew what all this meant,
or that it understood the depth of dying.
A stroke could make of me a God or devil,
or even both—effect as well as cause,
but each thing has its own eleventh hour,
and so I left it there. When I returned,
I saw the sum of mercy it had earned
by all its supplications and its prayers:
A silken angel, descended from its gauze,
had come down to minister and devour,
and bore its victim up the silver stairs.

   The following two poems (3 & 4) are from, "The Atomic Mother
Goose," a satirical collection of poems I wrote in the early 1970s. The
idea was to take the standard "Mother Goose" and use the forms to
create political poetry. I still like the idea.

3.

To Russia, To Russia, to bomb a fat city,
Home again, home again, lickety-splitty,
But what is it that glare that now meets our eyes?
I'll give you a clue: It's not the sunrise.

4.

Hickory, dickory, docket,
Up went a shining rocket,
On New York town it soon came down,
Hickory, dickory, docket.

Hickory, dickory, dare,
No children anywhere,
And after the bombs, no dads or moms,
Hickory, dickory, dare.

Hickory, dickory, doom,
Russia's just gone boom,
Who needed Moscow or New York anyhow?
Hickory, dickory, doom.

This poem was written about and is dedicated to Byron, Diana, Rebecca and Young Byron—dear friends and San Franciscans.

THE BROWN HOUSE

There is a house
on a hill,
tuxedoed in brown shingles,
the people brown inside it,
and all its studies brown.
There is Mr. Brown
a good man and true,
and Mrs. Brown,
lovely in mahogany,
and that tall young man Brown
with his rustbrown mustache
and the beautiful Brown girl
with long bronze hair,
whose eyes open like morning
under an amber sky.
Oh, Brown is my color,
the color of love,
and I love the Browns
in their chocolate house.
May the gods visit sweetness
on the Brown tree,
and on all its branches,
mocha, amber, mahogany, rust.